D1273976

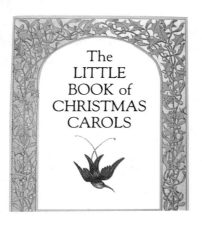

The LITTLE BOOK of CHRISTMAS CAROLS

RUNNING PRESS
PHILADELPHIA · LONDON

Contents

Introduction

The stamp of snowy shoes outside, a muffled giggle, silence, and then—a chorus of voices in the chill air, singing songs of the season. Caroling has a place at the heart of our holiday celebrations.

The tradition of caroling dates back five hundred years to the English "waits," groups of minstrels given the privilege of walking the town at Christmastime, singing at houses and receiving gifts from the townspeople. More recently, caroling was taken up by groups of boys, often unskilled in singing—but demanding a tip nonetheless! Caroling as we know it today began in Victorian times and continues little changed.

Through the years, songs other than carols have been sung at Christmastime. Some of the songs we call carols are hymns or popular songs that celebrate the holiday season. Others are traditional tunes sung with more contemporary lyrics.

The songs sung by carolers have changed as much as caroling itself, but the joy of singing together at Christmastime remains as great as ever!

Angels We Have Heard on High

Angels we have heard
    on high,
  Sweetly singing o'er
    the plains;
And the mountains, in reply,
  Echoing their joyous strains:

CHORUS:
Gloria in excelsis Deo,
Gloria in excelsis Deo!

Shepherds, why this jubilee?
    Why your joyful
        strains prolong?
What the gladsome tidings be
    That inspire your
        heav'nly song?

CHORUS

continued

Come to Bethlehem and see
Him whose birth the
angels sing.
Come adore on bended knee
Christ the Lord, our
newborn King.

CHORUS

See Him in a manger laid,
  Whom the choirs of
    angels praise.
Mary, Joseph, lend your aid
  While our hearts in love
    we raise.

CHORUS

Away in a Manger

Away in a manger,
 no crib for a bed,
The little Lord Jesus
 laid down His sweet head.
The stars in the heavens
 looked down where He lay:
The little Lord Jesus,
 asleep in the hay.

The cattle are lowing.
  The baby awakes,
But little Lord Jesus,
  no crying He makes.
I love Thee, Lord Jesus!
  Look down from the sky,
And stay by my cradle
  till morning is nigh.

Deck the Halls

Deck the halls with boughs
    of holly.
  Fa la la la la, la la la la.
'Tis the season to be jolly.
  Fa la la la la, la la la la.
Don we now our gay apparel.
  Fa la la, la la la, la la la.

continued

Troll the ancient
    Yuletide carol:
  Fa la la la la, la la la la.

See the blazing Yule before us.
  Fa la la la la, la la la la.
Strike the harp and join
    the chorus.
  Fa la la la la, la la la la.
Follow me in merry measure—
  Fa la la, la la la, la la la—

While I tell of
    Yuletide treasure.
    Fa la la la la, la la la la.

Fast away the old year passes.
    Fa la la la la, la la la la.
Hail the new, ye lads and lasses.
    Fa la la la la, la la la la.
Sing we joyous, all together—
    Fa la la, la la la, la la la—
Heedless of the wind
    and weather.
    Fa la la la la, la la la la.

The First Noel

The first Noel
　　the angels did say
　Was to certain poor
　　shepherds
　　　in fields as they lay—
In fields where they lay,
　　keeping their sheep,
　On a cold winter's night
　　that was so deep.

CHORUS:
Noel, Noel, Noel, Noel,
Born is the King of Israel!

They lookèd up and saw a star,
   Shining in the East,
      but beyond them far.
And unto the Earth
     it gave great light,
And so it continued,
     both day and night.

CHORUS *continued*

And by the light
of that same star
Three Wise Men came
from country far.
To seek for a King
was their intent,
And to follow the star
wherever it went.

CHORUS

This star drew nigh
    to the northwest.
Over Bethlehem
    it took its rest,
And there it did
    both stop and stay
Right over the stable
    where Jesus lay.

CHORUS

continued

Then they did know
  and in wonder confide
That within that house
  a King did reside.
One entered in then,
  with his own eyes to see
And discovered the Babe
  in poverty.

CHORUS

Between the stalls
  of the oxen, forlorn,
 This Child on that cold night
   in truth was born.
And for want of a crib,
  Mary did Him lay
 In the depths of a manger
   amongst the hay.

CHORUS

continued

Then entered in
    all those Wise Men three,
  Fell reverently
    upon bended knee,
And offered there,
    in His presence,
  Gifts of gold and of myrrh
    and of frankincense.

CHORUS

God Rest Ye Merry, Gentlemen

God rest ye merry, gentlemen;
  Let nothing you dismay.
Remember, Christ our Savior
  Was born on Christmas Day,
To save us all from
    Satan's pow'r
  When we had gone astray.

CHORUS:
Oh, tidings of comfort
  and joy,
Comfort and joy,
Oh, tidings of comfort
  and joy!

'Twas in the town of Bethlehem
  This blessed Babe was born.
They laid Him in a manger
  Where oxen feed on corn,

continued

And Mary knelt
   and prayed to God
Upon that blessed morn.

CHORUS

From God our Heav'nly Father
   A host of angels came
Unto some certain shepherds
   With tidings of the same:
That there was born
   in Bethlehem
The Son of God by name.

CHORUS

"Fear not," then said the angels,
   "Let nothing you affright.
This day is born a Savior
   Of virtue, pow'r, and might—
To ransom you from
    Sin and Death
   And vanquish Satan quite."

CHORUS

continued

The shepherds, at these tidings,
   Rejoicèd much in mind,
And on that windy plain
    they left
   Their sleeping flocks behind,
And straight they went
    to Bethlehem,
   Their newborn King to find.

CHORUS

Now when they came
  to Bethlehem,
 Where our sweet Savior lay,
They found Him in a manger,
 Where oxen feed on hay.
His blessed Mother,
  kneeling down,
 Unto the Lord did pray.

CHORUS

continued

With sudden joy and gladness
  The shepherds were beguiled,
To see the King of Israel
  And Holy Mary mild.
With them, in cheerfulness
    and love
  Rejoice each mother's child!

CHORUS

Now to the Lord sing praises,
  All you within this place,
And in true loving
      brotherhood
  Each other now embrace,
For Christmas doth
    in all inspire
  A glad and cheerful face.

CHORUS

Good King Wenceslas

Good King Wenceslas
        looked out
    On the Feast of Stephen,
When the snow lay
        'round about,
    Deep and crisp and even.
Brightly shone the moon
        that night,

Though the frost was cruel,
When a poor man came in sight,
　　Gath'ring winter fuël.

"Hither, page, and stand by me!
　　If thou hast heard telling,
Yonder peasant—who is he?
　　Where and what
　　　　his dwelling?"
"Sire, he lives a
　　　　good league hence,
　　Underneath the mountain,

continued

Right against the forest fence
    By Saint Agnes' fountain."

"Bring me flesh and
    bring me wine!
  Bring me pine-logs hither!
Thou and I will see him dine
    When we bear them thither."
Page and monarch,
    forth they went;
  Forth they went together,

Through the rude wind's
   wild lament
 And the bitter weather.

"Sire, the night grows
   darker now,
 And the wind blows stronger.
Fails my heart—I know not how
 I can go much longer!"
"Mark my footsteps, my
   good page.
 Tread thou in them boldly.

continued

Thou shall feel this
   winter's rage
  Freeze thy blood less coldly."

In his master's steps he trod,
  Where the snow lay dinted.
Heat was in the very sod
  Which the Saint had printed.
Therefore, Christian men,
   be sure,
  Wealth or rank possessing,
Ye who now will bless the poor
  Shall yourselves find blessing.

Hark! The Herald Angels Sing

Hark! The herald angels sing,
   "Glory to the newborn King!
Peace on Earth and mercy mild,
   God and sinners reconciled."
Joyful all ye nations, rise!
   Join the triumph of the skies.
With th'angelic host, proclaim,
   "Christ is born in Bethlehem!"

continued

CHORUS:
Hark! The herald angels sing,
"Glory to the newborn King!"

Christ, by highest
    Heav'n adored;
    Christ, the everlasting Lord:
Late in time,
    behold Him come,
Offspring of
    the Virgin's womb.

Veiled in flesh the Godhead see.
  Hail th'Incarnate Deity
Pleased as Man
    with men to dwell—
  Jesus, our Emmanuel!

CHORUS

Mild He lays His glory by,
  Born that man
    no more may die,

continued

Born to raise the sons of Earth,
  Born to give
    them second birth.
Light and life to all He brings,
  Ris'n with healing
    in His wings.
Hail, the Sun of Righteousness!
  Hail, the Heav'n-born
    Prince of Peace!

CHORUS

The Holly
and the Ivy

The holly and the ivy
  Now are both well grown,
Of all the trees that are
    in the wood
   The holly bears the crown.

CHORUS:
The rising of the sun,
The running of the deer,
The playing of the
    merry organ,
The singing in the choir.

The holly bears a blossom
    As white as the lily flower,

continued

And Mary bore sweet
    Jesus Christ
  To be our sweet Saviour.

CHORUS

The holly bears a berry
  As red as any blood,
And Mary bore sweet
    Jesus Christ
  To do poor sinners good.

CHORUS

The holly bears a prickle
　As sharp as any thorn,
And Mary bore sweet
　　Jesus Christ
　On Christmas day in the morn.

CHORUS

The holly bears a bark
　As bitter as any gall,
And Mary bore sweet
　　Jesus Christ
　For to redeem us all.   *continued*

CHORUS

The holly and the ivy
  Now are both well grown,
Of all the trees that are
    in the wood
  The holly bears the crown.

It Came Upon the Midnight Clear

It came upon the
    midnight clear,
  That glorious song of old,
From angels bending near
    the Earth
  To touch their harps of gold:
"Peace on the Earth!

Good will to men,
From Heaven's
all-gracious King!"
The world in solemn
stillness lay
To hear the angels sing.

Still through the cloven skies
they come,
With seraphs' wings unfurled;
And still their heavenly
music floats

continued

O'er all the weary world.
Above its sad and lowly plains
  They bend on
    hovering wing.
And ever o'er its Babel sounds
  The blessed angels sing.

Yet with the woes of sin
    and strife,
  The world has suffered long.
Beneath the angels' strains
    have rolled

Two thousand years
   of wrong;
And man, at war with man,
   hears not
The love-song
   which they bring.
Oh, hush the noise,
   ye men of strife,
   And hear the angels sing!

And ye, beneath life's
   crushing load,

continued

Whose shoulders are
      bending low,
Who toil along
      the climbing way
   With painful steps, and slow—
Take heart! For comfort, hope,
      and joy
   Come swiftly on the wing.
Oh, rest beside the weary road
   And hear the angels sing!

For lo! The days
      are hast'ning on,

As prophets knew of old,
And with the
    ever-circling years
Comes 'round the
    time foretold,
When love shall reign,
    and men declare
The Prince of Peace
    their King;
And all the Earth send back
    the song
Which now the angels sing.

Jingle, Bells

Dashing through the snow
  In a one-horse open sleigh,
O'er the field we go,
  Laughing all the way.
Bells on bobtail ring,
  Making spirits bright.
What fun it is to laugh and sing
  A sleighing song tonight!

continued

CHORUS:
Jingle, bells! Jingle, bells!
Jingle all the way!
Oh, what fun it is to ride
In a one-horse
   open sleigh—hey!
Jingle, bells! Jingle, bells!
Jingle all the way!
Oh, what fun it is to ride
In a one-horse open sleigh!

A day or two ago,
  I thought I'd take a ride,
And soon Miss Fannie Bright
  Was seated by my side.
The horse was lean and lank,
  But hardly worth his hay.
He veered into a drifted bank
  And overturned the sleigh!

CHORUS

continued

Now the ground is white.
  Go for it while you're young.
Take the girls tonight
  And sing this sleighing song.
Just rent a bobtail'd bay,
  Two-forty for his speed.
Then hitch him to
  an open sleigh,
  And crack! you'll take
    the lead!

CHORUS

You won't mind the cold,
  The robe is thick and warm.
Snow falls on the road,
  Silv'ring every form,
The woods are dark and still.
  The horse is trotting fast.
He'll pull the sleigh
    around the hill
  And home again at last.

CHORUS

Jolly Old Saint Nicholas

Jolly old Saint Nicholas,
  Lean your ear this way.
Don't you tell a single soul
  What I'm going to say.
Christmas Eve is coming soon!
  Now, you dear old man,
Whisper what you'll
    bring to me.
Tell me, if you can. *continued*

— · 63 · —

When the clock is
	striking twelve,
	When I'm fast asleep,
Down the chimney
	broad and black
	With your pack you'll creep.
All the stockings you will find,
	Hanging in a row.
Mine will be the shortest one—
	You'll be sure to know.

Johnny wants a pair of skates.
  Mary wants a sled.
Susie wants a picture book—
  One she's never read.
Now I think I'll leave to you
  What to give the rest.
Choose for me,
    dear Santa Claus—
  You will know the best.

Joy to the World

Joy to the world!
    The Lord is come.
  Let Earth receive her King.
Let ev'ry heart
    prepare Him room,
  And Heav'n and Nature sing,
  And Heav'n and Nature sing,
  And Heav'n, and Heav'n
    and Nature sing. *continued*

Joy to the world!
    The Savior reigns.
  Let men their songs employ,
While fields and floods,
    rocks, hills, and plains
Repeat the sounding joy,
Repeat the sounding joy,
Repeat, repeat
    the sounding joy.

He rules the world
    with truth and grace
  And makes the nations prove
The glories of His
    righteousness
  And wonders of His love,
  And wonders of His love,
  And wonders, wonders
    of His love.

Oh Christmas Tree

Oh Christmas Tree,
    Oh Christmas Tree,
  With lush green boughs
    unchanging—
Green when the summer
    sun is bright,
  And when the forest's
    cold and white.

continued

Oh Christmas Tree,
      Oh Christmas Tree,
   With lush green boughs
      unchanging!

Oh Christmas Tree,
      Oh Christmas Tree,
   Here once again to awe us,
You bear round fruits
      of Christmas past,
   Spun out of silver,

gold, and glass.
Oh Christmas Tree,
Oh Christmas Tree,
Here once again to awe us!

Oh Christmas Tree,
Oh Christmas Tree,
We gladly bid you welcome.
A pyramid of light you seem,
A galaxy of stars that gleam.
[Repeat first two lines.]

continued

Oh Christmas Tree,
    Oh Christmas Tree,
  You fill the air
    with fragrance.
You shrink to very tiny size,
  Reflected in
    the children's eyes.
[Repeat first two lines.]

Oh Christmas Tree,
    Oh Christmas Tree,
  What presents do
    you shelter?
Rich wrappings hide
    the gifts from sight,
Done up in bows
    and ribbons tight.
[Repeat first two lines.]

continued

Oh Christmas Tree,
    Oh Christmas Tree,
   Your green limbs teach
    a lesson:
That constancy
    and faithful cheer
  Are gifts to cherish
    all the year.
[Repeat first two lines.]

Oh Come, All Ye Faithful

Oh come, all ye faithful,
  Joyful and triumphant,
Oh come ye, oh come ye
    to Bethlehem.
  Come and behold Him,
    born the King of Angels.

continued

CHORUS:
Oh come, let us adore Him,
Oh come, let us adore Him,
Oh come, let us adore Him,
Christ the Lord!

Sing, choirs of angels,
    Sing in exultation.
Oh Sing, all ye citizens
    of Heav'n above:
"Glory to God,
    glory in the highest."

CHORUS

Oh True God of True God,
  Light of Light eternal,
Lo! He abhors not
    the Virgin's womb.
  Son of the Father,
    begotten not created.

CHORUS

continued

Yea, Lord, we greet Thee,
   Born this happy morning.
Jesus, to Thee all glory be giv'n,
   Word of the Father,
      now in flesh appearing.

CHORUS

Oh Little Town
of Bethlehem

Oh little town of Bethlehem,
  How still we see thee lie!
Above thy deep
    and dreamless sleep
  The silent stars go by.
Yet in thy dark streets shineth
  The everlasting light:

The hopes and fears
   of all the years
 Are met in thee tonight.

For Christ is born of Mary,
   And gathered all above,
While mortals sleep,
   the angels keep
 Their watch
   of wond'ring love.

continued

Oh, morning stars together,
  Proclaim the holy birth,
And praises sing
  to God the King,
  And peace to men on Earth.

Silent Night

Silent night, holy night!
  All is calm, all is bright
'Round yon Virgin
    Mother and Child—
  Holy infant,
    so tender and mild.
Sleep in heavenly peace,
Sleep in heavenly peace.

continued

Silent night, holy night!
Shepherds quake at the sight.
Glories stream
from Heaven afar,
Heav'nly hosts sing "Alleluia,
Christ the Savior is born,
Christ the Savior is born!"

Silent night, holy night!
Son of God, love's pure light,
Radiance beams from
Thy holy face,

With the dawn of
   redeeming grace.
Jesus, Lord at Thy birth,
Jesus, Lord at Thy birth!

The Twelve Days of Christmas

On the first day of Christmas,
  My true love gave to me
A partridge in a pear tree.

On the second day
    of Christmas,
  My true love gave to me
Two turtle doves,
    and a partridge in a pear tree.

On the third day of Christmas,
   My true love gave to me
Three French hens,
Two turtle doves,
   and a partridge in a pear tree.

On the fourth day
   of Christmas...
Four calling birds,...

On the fifth day
   of Christmas...
Five golden rings;...   *continued*

On the sixth day
of Christmas...
Six geese a-laying,...

On the seventh day
of Christmas...
Seven swans a-swimming,...

On the eighth day
of Christmas...
Eight maids a-milking,...

continued

On the ninth day
   of Christmas...
Nine ladies dancing,...

On the tenth day
   of Christmas...
Ten lords a-leaping,...

On the eleventh day
   of Christmas...
Eleven pipers piping,...

continued

On the twelfth day
   of Christmas,
  My true love gave to me
Twelve drummers drumming,
Eleven pipers piping,
Ten lords a-leaping,
Nine ladies dancing,
Eight maids a-milking,
Seven swans a-swimming,
Six geese a-laying,
Five golden rings;
Four calling birds,

Three French hens,
Two turtle doves,
And a partridge in a pear tree.

Up on the Rooftop

Up on the rooftop,
   reindeer pause.
 Out jumps good old
   Santa Claus!
Down through the chimney,
   with lots of toys—
 All for the little ones'
   Christmas joys.

continued

CHORUS:
Ho, ho, ho! Who
    wouldn't go?
Ho, ho, ho! Who
    wouldn't go
Up on the rooftop—
    Click, click, click!—
Down through the chimney
    with good St. Nick?

First comes the stocking
    of little Nell.
  Oh, dear Santa, fill it well!
Give her a dolly
    that laughs and cries,
  One that can open
    and shut her eyes.

CHORUS

continued

Next hangs the stocking
    of brother Will.
  It won't take
    very much to fill—
Give him a hammer
    and lots of tacks,
Plus a red ball
    and a whip that cracks.

CHORUS

Reindeer are restless
    beside your sleigh,
Eager to leave
    and be on their way.
But on the mantel,
    I've left for you
Apples, an orange,
    and warm milk too.

CHORUS

continued

Last is a stocking
    that's deep and strong—
I've been a good boy
    all year long!
Please, if you have them,
    and if they'll fit,
Give me a bat
    and a catcher's mitt.

CHORUS

We Three Kings of Orient Are

We three kings of Orient are.
   Bearing gifts,
      we traverse afar—
Field and fountain,
      moor and mountain—
   Following yonder star.

CHORUS:
Oh, star of wonder,
   star of night,
Star of royal beauty bright,
Westward leading,
   still proceeding,
Guide us to thy
   perfect light.

continued

[MELCHIOR:]
Born a king
    on Bethlehem's plain—
Gold I bring,
    to crown Him again—
King for ever, ceasing never,
Over us all to reign.

CHORUS

[GASPAR:]
Frankincense
    to offer have I.
  Incense owns a Deity nigh.
Prayer and praising,
    all men raising,
Worship Him,
    God most high!

CHORUS

continued

[BALTHAZAR:]
Myrrh is mine:
    its bitter perfume
Breathes a life
    of gathering gloom,
Sorrowing, sighing,
    bleeding, dying,
Sealed in the
    stone-cold tomb.

CHORUS

[ALL:]
Glorious now,
    behold Him arise:
  King and God and sacrifice!
Heav'n sings, "*Ha*-le-lu-ia!"
    "*Ha*-ah-le-
  Lu-ia!" the Earth replies.

CHORUS

We Wish You a Merry Christmas

We wish you
   a Merry Christmas,
We wish you
   a Merry Christmas,
We wish you
   a Merry Christmas
And a Happy New Year!

continued

CHORUS:
Glad tidings we bring
To you and your kin.
We wish you
    a Merry Christmas,
And a Happy New Year.

Oh, bring us
    some figgy pudding,
Oh, bring us
    some figgy pudding,

Oh, bring us
   some figgy pudding
And a glass of good cheer!

CHORUS

We won't go until we get some,
   We won't go
      until we get some,
We won't go until we get some
   So bring it right here!

CHORUS   *continued*

We'll sing you
    some happy carols,
We'll sing you
    some happy carols,
We'll sing you
    some happy carols
To ravish your ear!

CHORUS

We have quite
    the finest voices,
We have quite
    the finest voices,
We have quite
    the finest voices
That you'll ever hear!

CHORUS

continued

We wish you
    a Merry Christmas,
We wish you
    a Merry Christmas,
We wish you
    a Merry Christmas
And a Happy New Year!

What Child is This?

What Child is this who,
    laid to rest,
 On Mary's lap is sleeping;
Whom angels greet
    with anthems sweet,
    While shepherds watch
    are keeping?

continued

Chorus:
This, this is Christ the King,
Whom shepherds guard
  and angels sing.
Haste, haste
  to bring Him laud,
The Babe, the Son of Mary.

Why lies He in
  such mean estate,
Where ox and ass
  are feeding?

Good Christian,
  fear for sinners here,
  The silent Word is pleading.

CHORUS

So bring Him incense,
  gold, and myrrh.
Come, peasants, kings,
  to own Him.

continued

The King of Kings
    salvation brings—
Let loving hearts
    enthrone Him!

The old year now away is fled,
The New Year now
    is enterèd.

Then let us now
    our sins downtread,
And joyfully all appear.

NEW CHORUS:
Merry be the holiday,
And let us run
    with sport and play.
Hang sorrow, cast care away.
God send you a Happy
    New Year!

continued

— · 123 · —

And now, best wishes
all good friends
Unto each other
they do send.
Oh, grant we may
our lives amend,
And have no one's blame
to fear.

NEW CHORUS

This book has been bound using handcraft methods, and Smyth-sewn to ensure durability.

The text was edited by Peter Siegenthaler.

The dust jacket was designed by Toby Schmidt.

The interior was designed by Stephanie Longo.

The illustrations were researched by Gillian Speeth. The illustrations on pages 1, 13, 14, 25, 38, 49, 57, 66, 81, 90, 96, 117, 118, and 125 are courtesy the Popular Culture Library, Bowling Green State University. Those on pages 56, 84, and 110 are provided by The Granger Collection, New York. Those on pages 1, 70, 87, 93, and 95 are provided by Hulton/Bettman. The illustrations on pages 7, 43, 62, and 103 are taken from Margaret and Kenn Whitmyer, *Christmas Collectibles*, Collector Books, Paducah, KY, 1987.

The text was typeset in Goudy Oldstyle by Commcor Communications Corporation, Philadelphia, Pennsylvania.